To Christine, Kathleen, and Jennifer—
wouldn't this have been a fun trip to take!
Love you forever, Mom

A hardcover edition of this book was originally published in 2005
by Chronicle Books LLC.

Text © 2005 by Toni Trent Parker.
Illustrations © 2005 by Janell Genovese.
All rights reserved.

Book design by Sara Gillingham.
Typeset in Ruly and Skryptaag.
The illustrations in this book were rendered in mixed media.
Manufactured in China.

Library of Congress Cataloging-in-Publication Data
Parker, Toni Trent.
Sienna's scrapbook: our African American heritage trip /
by Toni Trent Parker ; illustrated by Janell Genovese.
p. cm.
Summary: A young girl's parents take her and her brother
on a summer trip to visit the sites of African American history.
ISBN 0-8118-5420-5
1. African Americans—Juvenile fiction.
[1. African Americans—Fiction.]
I. Genovese, Janell, ill. II. Title.
PZ7.P237Si 2005
[Fic]—dc22
2004026426

Distributed in Canada by Raincoast Books
9050 Shaughnessy Street, Vancouver, British Columbia V6P 6E5

10 9 8 7 6 5 4 3 2 1

Chronicle Books LLC
85 Second Street, San Francisco, California 94105

www.chroniclekids.com

Sienna's Scrapbook

Our African American Heritage Trip

by Toni Trent Parker

with illustrations by Janell Genovese

chronicle books · san francisco

July 13, Hartford, Conn.

Drat! Here it is, summer vacation, and my parents have already ruined it. I was going to spend this year's family reunion hangin' with my cousins, biking around Winston-Salem, swimming in Uncle Buddy's pond, and, of course, eating lots of those hot, delicious doughnuts straight from the Krispy Kreme bakery. Now they have this idea that we should stop off and visit black historical sites on our drive down to North Carolina so that my little brother, Davey, and I can learn about our heritage. Ugh! Summer is supposed to be about fun, not about learning!

We start our trip tomorrow. It's going to be a looooong drive with all those stops.

Bring for trip ✿

notebook
pencils
paints
markers
sharpener
snacks
pillow
camera
film

my Family Trip

me

Hartford

grandma grandpa

Winston Salem

The first will be New Haven, to see the replica of a ship named the *Amistad*. "A replica is a copy," Dad told us. The real *Amistad* was sold way back in 1840, and nobody knows what happened to it after 1844. But in 1839, the *Amistad* was carrying African slaves when some of them rebelled, killed the captain and the cook, and took over the ship.

Davey—he's only six—was really excited about seeing a "giant sailboat."

"It's not a sailboat," I told him. "It's a schooner."

you don't have to hear Davey so I

AMISTAD

I already knew a little about the *Amistad* because I saw the movie, but boy, was I surprised when I saw the ship. It's so small! I was expecting something huge, since it carried almost sixty people—fifty-three Africans, plus five crew members. The guide told us the *Amistad* hadn't been used as a slave ship before—it was a cargo ship, meant to carry things like sugarcane.

We went down below the main deck to see where the Africans had been kept. This replica had a nice wood floor so we could walk on it, but the real *Amistad* didn't have a floor, just sand at the bottom of the cargo area to collect any water that leaked in. On top of the sand were piles of supplies. The Africans had to sit on top of the piles. There wasn't even enough room left for them to sit up straight. And they were chained together. How horrible! I sure wouldn't last long in a space like that.

Four of the slaves were children—can you *believe* that?! All under the age of ten. I guess the captain didn't think they could make much trouble, because they were allowed to stay on the deck during the trip. One of the kids was a girl called Margru. Later, an American friend gave her the name Sarah.

Margru returned to Sierra Leone in 1841 with thirty-four of the other Africans who had been aboard the *Amistad*. All the others had died. She lived with an American missionary family there. And do you know what? In 1846, when she was fifteen years old, she sailed back to America. Imagine that! She came back to the country where she'd been put in prison and where slavery was still legal. That was awfully brave. She went to Oberlin College in Ohio. Then, in 1849, she returned to Africa to start a girls' school.

Margru

Back on the main deck, Davey found a trapdoor. "What's this?" he yelled, and everybody turned to stare at us. It turned out to be the entrance to a tiny cage where slaves were put for punishment. It's called a *lazarette*, and I couldn't believe a grown-up could ever fit into it. I sure hope nobody was put there—though I have to say, sometimes it would be nice to have a cage for Davey!

Our guide told us that the Africans on the *Amistad* had been brought across the Atlantic Ocean on a large slave ship with other slaves. When it landed in Cuba, fifty-three slaves were put on the *Amistad* to be brought to the other side of Cuba, where they would be taken to work on a sugarcane plantation.

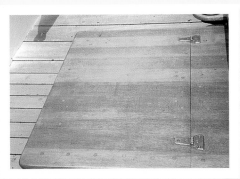

But one of the Africans—a man named Cinque—saw the ship's cook make a motion with his hand like he was slicing his own throat. Cinque thought the man was telling him that the Africans were going to be killed and then cooked! And that's what led to the revolt. I sure don't blame them! I'd revolt too if I thought someone was going to cook me.

The Africans kept three of the crew members alive to help them sail back to Africa. During the day, they *did* sail toward Africa, because the Africans knew that their home was in the direction of the rising sun. But each night, after the sun had set, the Spanish crew turned the ship around and sailed toward the coast of the United States.

This is the Amistad under full sail. WOW!

They zig-zagged back and forth like this for two months, but since the trip around Cuba was only supposed to have taken six days, they had food for only a week. They must have gotten awfully hungry. In the end the ship was captured by the U.S. Navy and towed to New London, Connecticut, where the Africans were put on trial for murder. Imagine that! They'd been stolen from their own homes, and now they were on trial for killing the people who stole them.

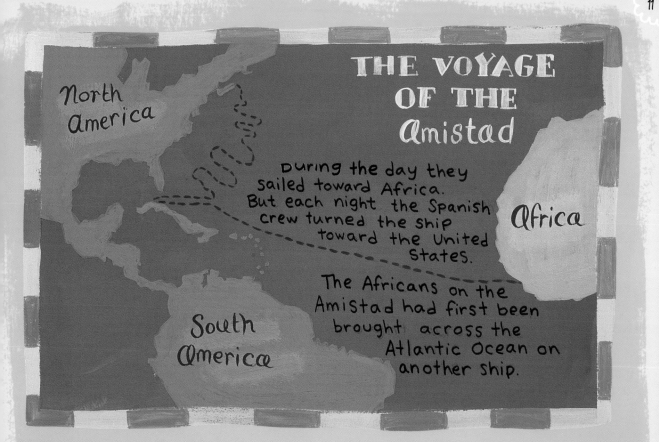

THE VOYAGE OF THE Amistad

During the day they sailed toward Africa. But each night the Spanish crew turned the ship toward the United States.

The Africans on the Amistad had first been brought across the Atlantic Ocean on another ship.

North America

Africa

South America

The trial was a really big thing. The abolitionists, people who were against slavery, said the Africans were free men who were only trying to get back home. But the U.S. government said they were slaves with no freedom and no right to demand it. The case went all the way to the Supreme Court. And the Supreme Court agreed with the abolitionists! They said the Africans on board the Amistad were free people who had been kidnapped, and they were free to go back to Africa. Way to go!!!

Well, that was pretty interesting. We're heading to New York City now. Mom says we'll be there for two days and won't see even half of what's there to see. Oh, for a Krispy Kreme!

July 15, New York City

N.Y.C.

Dad played a lot of *his* favorite CDs on the trip down to New York—Louis Armstrong, Duke Ellington, Bessie Smith, Billie Holiday. He said he's getting us ready for our introduction to the Harlem Renaissance, and this music was popular then, in the 1920s and '30s. Of course, Davey and I wanted to hear our music, not Dad's.

The traffic in New York City sure is different from Hartford's! There are so many taxis and bikers driving crazy all over the road and lots of buses and tons of people crossing the street everywhere. Poor Dad—he had to go slow and be extra careful. We couldn't wait to get out of the car and start exploring the city.

125th Street, which is also called Martin Luther King Jr. Boulevard in Harlem, is a lot busier than I expected. This street really moves. It's full of small shops and tables on the sidewalk selling everything from hair dyes to books. Davey was excited to see a book he had at home about Jamal and his busy day at school. Of course, he wanted Mom to buy him another copy.

It sounded like music was coming out of every store all up and down the street—some Latin, some rap, some gospel, and all of it LOUD! There were lots of stands with fruits and vegetables I'd never seen before, like pawpaw (which looks like papaya), christophene (which is like a squash), cassava, and passion fruit. Mom said a lot of people from the Caribbean live in Harlem, and these are Caribbean foods.

As we walked around, Mom told us about all the famous writers and artists who were a part of the Harlem Renaissance, like Langston Hughes, Countee Cullen, Zora Neale Hurston, Augusta Savage, and Jacob Lawrence. Dad thinks Harlem is going through a second renaissance because of all the new businesses and stores opening.

Renaissance means rebirth. Neat, huh? A part of a city getting reborn. Harlem is a New York neighborhood where Blacks have lived for a long time.

Langston Hughes

Langston Hughes was a poet and novelist. He created a character called Simple to tell his stories about life in Harlem. Countee Cullen was a big-time poet. Zora Neale Hurston wrote *Their Eyes Were Watching God* and a lot of other books. Augusta Savage was an important sculptor, and Jacob Lawrence was a painter. He is especially famous for a series of sixty paintings about the migration of Blacks from the South to the North during the Great Depression.

HARLEM
RENAISSANCE

MAP
POSTER
GUIDE

An Illustrated Map:

- Homes of Musicians, Artists & Writers
- Civil Rights Sites
- The Legendary Nightclubs

Dad got us a map that showed all the important spots in Harlem.

Davey REALLY wants to take a subway ride.

JAMAL'S BUSY DAY

by Wade Hudson
illustrated by George Ford

Davey's book

EVIDENCE!!!

Duke Ellington

This is Duke Ellington. He was a famous composer and bandleader and piano player. He composed stuff with funny titles like "Satin Doll" and "Cottontail."

We walked over to 8th Avenue (in Harlem it's also called Frederick Douglass Boulevard), and you'll never guess what we found! A Krispy Kreme store! Awesome! I thought you could only get Krispy Kremes in the South, but the woman behind the counter told us there are Krispy Kreme stores in lots of states now—even in Connecticut. Wow! I sure didn't know that. We got a dozen glazed doughnuts, and they were gone in four minutes flat. They are the best!

After all the Krispy Kremes we'd eaten, I didn't think I could eat another thing—but that was before we got to Sylvia's world-famous restaurant. *Everyone* eats at Sylvia's. I mean it. Spike Lee. Danny Glover. TLC. Beyoncé. LL Cool J. Jay-Z. Because Sylvia is "the Queen of Soul Food." She is famous for her collard greens, pinto beans, tuna croquettes, and of course, fried chicken. I had chicken, greens, and macaroni and cheese, and banana pudding for dessert. Sylvia's mac and cheese was better than Mom's, but I'll never tell that to Mom!

The restaurant was crowded, even though it was the middle of the week. The walls were covered with photographs of all the famous people who've eaten there. I kept hoping someone famous would come in while *we were* there. Mom says Bill Clinton, who used to be president and now lives in New York, comes a lot—after all, he is from the South. Too bad he didn't come tonight.

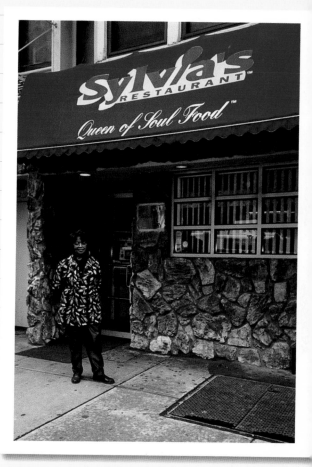

↑

We met Sylvia (Mrs. Sylvia Woods, the owner), and I took a picture of her outside the restaurant. When I told her how great her mac and cheese was, she gave me her recipe to take home. Wow!

July 16, New York City

This morning, we took the subway to Queens to see the home of Louis Armstrong, one of Dad's favorite trumpet players. (Dad is big on music—can't you tell?) Mr. Armstrong played all over the world, even for kings and queens, and he recorded thousands of songs. But you know what? He lived in a very small house. I would have thought his house would be huge since he was so famous, but our living room at home is much bigger than his.

Dad loved seeing Mr. Armstrong's gold records and his trumpet, and Mom couldn't get over the wallpaper. Mrs. Armstrong was really into wallpaper—she papered every wall, some of the ceilings, and even the closets! Davey liked the goldfish in the little pond in the backyard. But what I liked best were the special sound effects. In several of the rooms, the guide touched the wall and music came on. Just like magic! The guide told us the music wasn't there when the Armstrongs lived there—it was added when the house was fixed up for tours.

My dad—the jazz professor!

This is Louis Armstrong's den. He kept two tape recorders there, and he recorded lots of his daily conversations. He even took a tape recorder with him on the road and recorded conversations there too—even talks with hotel maids and bellmen. Wow!

the APOLLO

Tonight we went to Amateur Night at the Apollo. Amateur Night was started when the Apollo first opened in 1934. On one night each week, unknown people can perform there and hopefully get a start in show business. Ella Fitzgerald, James Brown, and Lauryn Hill all sang on Amateur Night before they were famous.

The theater was packed. There were lots of Japanese tourists in the audience. The first two performers were both ten-year-old girls! Boy, were they brave. I could never, ever get up on stage and sing—I'd be too nervous. But they were really good.

The first thing all the performers did when they came on stage was rub their hands on the Tree of Hope, which was on the stage. The story goes that this tree grew near the Lafayette Theater, which was THE theater in Harlem during the 1920s and '30s. Some performers thought the tree brought them good luck if they stood underneath it. So, when the tree had to be cut down when the street was fixed up, part of the tree trunk was brought to the Apollo and put onstage to bring good luck to its performers. How cool is that?

The other entertainers tonight were adults, and the audience got their say on which ones they liked or disliked. They cheered and clapped like crazy if they liked the performer, and they booed if they didn't. At first I thought that was pretty rude, but each time the audience booed, this funny-looking character called "the executioner" stumbled across the stage, did some flips, acted silly, and "swept" the singer off the stage with a broom. He was so funny, I even saw performers who were being swept away smile!

AMATEUR NIGHT

AP0910 C.ORCH O 100
$24.00 INC $2.FAC CHRG
CONVENIENCE CHARGE
SECTION C.ORCH
MC 9X
ROW O 100
APT404A AT THE APOLLO THEA
AMATEUR NIGHT
REGULAR SHOW
APOLLO THEATE
253 W 125TH STREET,

Me on stage at the Apollo . . .
IN MY DREAMS!!!

New York City is really exciting. This is definitely a place I want to visit again. Tomorrow we're off to Philadelphia. This "heritage trip" isn't turning out so bad after all!

July 17, Philadelphia, Pa.

Did Mom ever have a surprise for us today—she took us to a doll museum! I thought the only museums Mom liked were art museums. "I found a black-doll museum on the Internet, and I thought you kids might like to go," she told us. Boy, would I! Davey wasn't so sure.

When we got to the museum, I couldn't believe my eyes. There were more than 300 black dolls inside. Small dolls and big dolls—there was one almost as tall as Davey. Cloth dolls, wood dolls, plastic dolls, and some really old dolls made out of porcelain and papier mâché. There were also "folk dolls" made out of corn husks, nuts, and bottles! I had no idea there were so many different types of dolls. Some of the really old, old dolls were made out of straw. The beaded dolls from South Africa were great. Davey found the Fat Albert and Tuskegee Airman dolls right away, of course.

One collection of dolls was all dressed in white. They'd been made in Germany in the early 1900s. The museum owner told us that Germany was the leading doll-making country at that time, and the Germans were the first to start making "exotic" dolls—that's what they called black dolls then.

The owner has been collecting dolls for more than twenty years, mainly at antique shows and flea markets and through doll catalogs. "In the 1930s and '40s, most of the black dolls were white dolls that were painted brown," she told us. "It wasn't until the 1950s that more ethnic-looking dolls appeared."

We stayed at the museum for over an hour, and I didn't want to leave then. What I really wanted to do was take a couple hundred of the dolls home with me.

A Tuskegee Airman Doll →

Next, we went to see the Johnson House in a section of Philadelphia called Germantown. (It's named that because it's where many Germans lived when they came here long ago.) This is one of the very few homes on the Underground Railroad that is open to the public. Many of the other homes used as "station stops" during slavery are used as homes today.

"How did the slaves see to escape if everything was under-ground?" Davey asked. I didn't laugh, because when I first heard about the Underground Railroad, I thought it was below ground, too. It's not, though. This "railroad" was actually a lot of hiding places where slaves hid in their escape from the South, going from one to another until they reached the North, where slavery was no longer allowed. Almost any place could be used as a station stop—a home, a church, a barn. But everything had to be a secret because if the slaves were caught, they would be returned to their owners and severely punished.

The front door of the Johnson House was funny—it was split in half. It was made that way to keep animals out and let air in at the same time.

This is the door to the "secret" room.

This is the outbuilding where slaves were also hidden.

The house was part of a 300-acre farm owned by a Quaker family. Many Quakers, a group of Christians, thought slavery was wrong, so they set up stations on the Underground Railroad. In one of the rooms, we saw an ankle collar and chains like the ones used to chain the slaves together. Davey and I picked up the chains. They were really heavy.

We went up to the third floor to see the room where the slaves were hidden. It was tiny, with no windows, but it wasn't really hidden, just behind a door like any other.

Candles were placed in the upstairs windows to let slaves know that this was a safe house where they could hide for the day. The Johnsons also hid slaves in another building on their farm and in a storage room.

"The Underground Railroad was a network of people helping people," Dad said.

That was nice of people to help the slaves reach freedom, but it would have been better if there had been no slavery at all.

July 18, Philadelphia

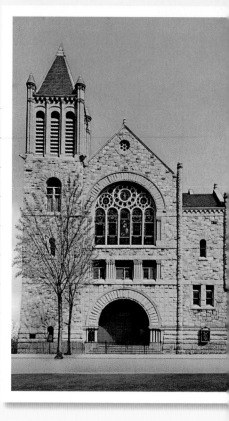

"What better way to learn about our history than to see the real places?" said Dad. He didn't bother to mention that our next stop was going to be a church.

The church was the Mother Bethel AME Church (AME stands for "African Methodist Episcopal"), which was started in 1797 by Richard Allen, a Philadelphia slave who had bought his freedom. He also founded the Free African Society, the first black organization dedicated to helping people of color.

After purchasing his freedom in 1780, Richard Allen became a traveling preacher. He was so popular that he was preaching all over Philadelphia. But segregation was getting stronger and stronger. In 1786 he was asked to come preach to the black members of the mainly white St. George's Methodist Episcopal Church in Philadelphia—at five o'clock in the morning! You'd never see me up that early!

Then, one Sunday, while he and other Blacks were sitting in the balcony and praying, one of the white members of the church told them to move to the back of the balcony. Richard Allen and some of the others left the church and decided to organize their own church to serve all the black people who lived in the area. He organized the Bethel African Methodist Episcopal Church, and the word *Mother* was added on later after lots of other Bethel AME churches were organized in other cities. The church was also a station on the Underground Railroad.

AFRICA Nubia

Mom dragged us off to another museum this afternoon, but there were no dolls in it. Too bad. It was called the African American Museum in Philadelphia. There was an exhibit about ancient Egypt and Nubia when we were there. Nubia was the land next to Egypt. The black Kingdom of Kush was located there.

We saw a bronze Nubian ax blade that was several *thousand* years old! And there was something called a kohl stick that Nubian women used to apply eye makeup. I never knew they had makeup way back then. We saw some hieroglyphs that the ancient Africans used to communicate with each other. There was a rubbing station for kids, so Davey and I got to do some rubbings of the symbols for *water* and *child*. That was pretty cool.

Upstairs, there was a display of some small decorated boxes that the artist, Martina Johnson–Allen, called Memory Boxes. She had painted some of her memories on pieces of paper, then attached them to the boxes. They were neat! When I get home, I'm going to make a Memory Box of this trip.

Davey got a little restless and started running up and down the ramp in the museum until the guard came over and told him that wasn't allowed. So Dad took him outside and bought him a Philly pretzel with mustard on it. Sounds pretty awful to me, but he loved it!

July 19, Baltimore, Md.

Davey is such a pest! Today he decided to spread out all his toy space men on the back seat. He has about thirty of them. What a mess. Dad started playing his CDs in the car again. This time, he played the music of Eubie Blake and Cab Calloway, who were born in Baltimore. (He likes to get us ready for the cities we are visiting musically.)

As soon as we got to Baltimore, we went to the Great Blacks in Wax Museum, and it was great! It was packed with wax figures of so many famous black Americans, from Harriet Tubman and Booker T. Washington to great musicians like Billie Holiday and Eubie Blake (the same musicians on Dad's CDs!) to people who are alive today, like Colin Powell and Nelson Mandela. Davey got really excited about the figures of Bill Pickett, the rodeo star, and Matthew Henson, the Arctic explorer. I think what he liked best was the huge polar bear next to Mr. Henson. I really liked the "Great Women in Civil Rights" display, which included figures of Rosa Parks, Fannie Lou Hamer, and Shirley Chisholm—because I'm a girl, of course!

Bill Pickett

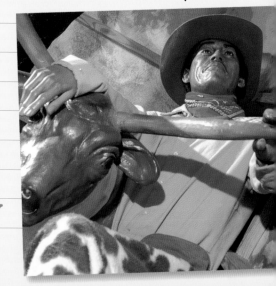

In 1955, Rosa Parks refused to give up her seat on a Montgomery, Alabama, bus. She was arrested, and today she is called "the Mother of the Civil Rights Movement." Fannie Lou Hamer organized voter registration drives in Mississippi in the 1960s and demanded the right to participate as a Mississippi delegate at the Democratic National Convention in 1964. In 1968, Shirley Chisholm was the first African American woman elected to the U.S. Congress. She was also the first black woman to run for the office of president of the United States.

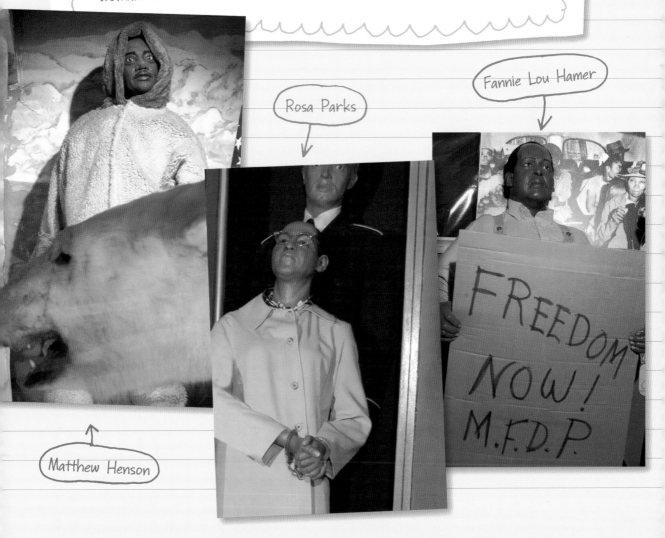

Rosa Parks

Fannie Lou Hamer

Matthew Henson

FREEDOM NOW! M.F.D.P.

After the wax museum, Mom and Dad took us to the Gospel Music Crab Feast, and boy was that food *good*. Maryland is famous for crabs, so we ate a pile of crab cakes and tons of cooked crabs. We had to use these tiny picks to get the crab meat out of the crab shells. It was messy and a lot of work, but it sure was worth it. And, while we were eating, all this wonderful gospel music was being performed. There was also a skit on the life of Harriet Tubman, who was born in Maryland.

Tomorrow we head off to Washington, D.C. We'll stay there three days because Dad says there are so many exciting things to see there.

July 20, Washington, D.C.

Well, Dad was right—the minute we drove into Washington, Davey and I were *glued* to the windows so we wouldn't miss anything. The Lincoln and Jefferson memorials, the Washington Monument, the Capitol, the White House—WOW! We could hardly wait to get checked in to the hotel so we could go right back out again.

Our first stop was the Lincoln Memorial. It was awesome. It's supposed to look like a Greek temple, and it has thirty-six columns— one for each state that was part of the United States in 1865, the year Lincoln was assassinated. The statue of Lincoln sitting in a chair is gigantic, and the words of his Gettysburg Address and Second Inaugural Address are engraved on the inside of the memorial.

"Two very important events in black history took place here," said Mom. She told us about the Marian Anderson concert in 1939. Marian Anderson was a famous opera singer. She wanted to give a concert at Constitution Hall in Washington, but the Daughters of the American Revolution, who owned the hall, refused to let her use it because she was black. That was pretty awful! So U.S. Secretary of the Interior Harold Ickes, invited her to sing at the Lincoln Memorial, and she did. A huge crowd came to hear her. And guess what? My grandfather, who worked for Secretary Ickes, went to the concert! He even saved the program.

The other important African American event at the Lincoln Memorial took place in August 1963, when Dr. Martin Luther King Jr. led the March on Washington to protest the conditions of black Americans. He gave his famous "I Have a Dream" speech at the Lincoln Memorial. Davey and I know that speech well because every Martin Luther King Day, Dad sits us down and plays a tape of the speech for us to hear. I could hardly believe I was standing on the *exact same* spot where Dr. King stood when he gave that speech. There is an actual engraving on the step. As I stood on it, I imagined a crowd of more than 200,000 people looking at me just as they looked at him. It was pretty amazing.

I HAVE A DREAM
MARTIN LUTHER KING JR.
THE MARCH ON WASHINGTON
FOR JOBS AND FREEDOM
AUGUST 28, 1963

Grandpa let me make a copy
of the program for my scrapbook.

Howard University and Associated Sponsors

PRESENT

MARIAN ANDERSON

AT

THE LINCOLN MEMORIAL

IN

WASHINGTON

Sunday, April 9, 1939

FIVE O'CLOCK

*"Fourscore and seven years ago our fathers brought forth on
this continent a new nation, conceived in liberty and dedicated
to the proposition that all men are created equal."*

ABRAHAM LINCOLN.

Sitting for Justice: The Greensboro Sit-in of 1960

We got on a Tourmobile, which is a trolley that takes people up and down the National Mall area, and we went to the National Museum of American History. The first thing we saw was a lunch counter from a Woolworth's store. There was a sign above the counter that said you could buy a banana split for thirty-nine cents. Can you believe that! Thirty-nine cents! That was sure from the olden days.

Anyway, Dad told us why a lunch counter was in a museum. "For many years, Blacks in the South were not allowed to eat in the same restaurants as white people," he said. Blacks were allowed to cook and serve, but not to eat. Can you believe that?! So, one day in February 1960, four black students from North Carolina A&T College went to the Woolworth's in Greensboro, North Carolina, sat down at this lunch counter, and refused to move until they were served.

Well, of course, some of the white people didn't like that. The students were arrested. But this sit-in started a movement that led to big changes in civil rights all over the country.

"It took a lot of time, and many people died, both black and white," Dad told us. "But we have the rights we have today because of that movement. That's why this lunch counter is so important."

For once, Davey and I agreed on something—that ice cream was GOOD!

After that, I was ready for an ice cream, so we went down to the cafeteria and had a treat, but not a banana split.

Davey was getting cranky, so we left the museum to go back to our hotel. This time we took a taxi, which passed by the Capitol. Dad told us that slaves made up most of the workers who built the Capitol and the White House. "Slave owners were given five dollars per month for each slave who worked on the construction," he said. Imagine that—our government buildings were built by men who were not free. Not too cool.

July 21, Washington, D.C.

Our first stop today was the Air and Space Museum at the Smithsonian Institution. But by now I know that museums aren't just about art!

This place was really awesome. Airplanes and space capsules were hanging all over the place! The "Black Wings" exhibit was all about black aviators and astronauts, with lots of photographs of the Tuskegee Airmen, who fought in World War II. Davey remembered the Tuskegee Airman doll at the Doll Museum in Philadelphia, so he was really excited. And, of course, he loved all the airplanes.

Before World War II, Blacks in the military were assigned menial jobs as cooks, drivers, or laborers. But in 1941, the U.S. Army Air Corps (which later became the U.S. Air Force) opened a training center for pilots at the all-black Tuskegee Institute in Alabama. These pilots, known as the Tuskegee Airmen, flew combat missions during the war in North Africa and Italy. They flew escort planes for bombing raids into Germany and never lost a single bomber.

We saw a picture of Bessie Coleman, the first black woman aviator, and *Black Wings*, the book that Guion Bluford, the first black astronaut to go into space, took with him on his first mission in 1983. The book is a history of Blacks in aviation and is filled with lots of photos of the early black pilots. Davey says he wants to go into space. I think that's a great idea, especially if he goes today and stays for a year or two.

I bought some postcards in the gift shop to send to my cousins. Davey bought some freeze-dried ice cream that astronauts take into space with them.

Davey ATE the ice cream, of course! He let me keep the package for my scrapbook.

BYE!!!

FREEZE-DRIED
ICE CREAM
CHOCOLATE · VANILLA · STRAWBERRY
SPACE FOOD

TEAR HERE

READY TO EAT

NET WT. 3/4 OZ. (21g)

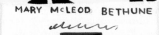

MARY McLEOD BETHUNE

This afternoon, we went to Lincoln Park. During the Civil War, the Lincoln Hospital was here. In 1867, two years after Lincoln was assassinated, Congress named it Lincoln Square. It was the first site named in his honor.

There is a sculpture here, called the Emancipation Statue, of a slave being freed by Lincoln. It was entirely paid for by freed slaves. Charlotte Scott, a former slave, used the first five dollars she ever earned in freedom to start raising money to pay for the statue.

Another statue in this park was built by the National Council of Negro Women as a memorial to Mary McLeod Bethune, their founder. The sculptor was Robert Berks, the African American artist who also sculpted the bust of President John F. Kennedy in the foyer of the John F. Kennedy Center for the Performing Arts.

In 1904, Mary McLeod Bethune started a school for black children in Florida. Eventually, that school became Bethune-Cookman College. Mrs. Bethune was also a member of President Franklin D. Roosevelt's "Black Cabinet," a group of distinguished black Americans who advised the president. She and Mrs. Eleanor Roosevelt became good friends.

It is soooo hot in Washington. Good thing our hotel has a pool. That's where I'm going right now.

July 22, Washington, D.C.

Today we went to the Frederick Douglass House, which sits way up on a hill with a great view of the city. The house has twenty-one rooms—can you believe that? Douglass moved there with his wife, Anna, in 1877, and the house is the way it was when he died in 1895. It's full of great stuff, like Abraham Lincoln's cane (Mrs. Lincoln gave it to Douglass) and a fantastic carved clock from Germany. There was a really old typewriter on a table in Mrs. Douglass's sewing room. I'm sure they thought typewriters were the greatest invention in the olden days, but boy, would Mrs. Douglass be surprised if she could see how a computer can type!

Frederick Douglass
National Historic Site

National Parks Passport Series 1992

What Davey remembers most about the house is what scared him most—Mr. Douglass's death mask. It seems pretty weird, but in the old days, molds were made of the faces of important people when they died, I guess to preserve their images for history. It really is kind of spooky.

Frederick Douglass was born a slave in 1818, but he escaped to freedom when he was twenty years old. It was illegal to educate slaves, but when he was still a child, Douglass learned to read by trading bread for reading lessons. When he grew up, he was an abolitionist, an author, a newspaper editor, and the most respected African American speaker of the time.

FREDERICK DOUGLASS
"What To The Slave Is The 4th Of July?"

Rochester, New York, July 5, 1852

Frederick Douglass, a leading Abolitionist and celebrated human rights leader, was born a slave in Maryland in 1818. As a child, Douglass secretly learned to read and write (it was against the law for a slave to do so). After escaping to freedom in 1838, he devoted himself to the Abolitionist cause. A brilliant speaker, Douglass drew on his own personal struggles to drive home his anti-slavery message.

In 1845, Douglass published his autobiography, Narrative of the Life of Frederick Douglass, An American Slave, which has endured as a classic in American literature. He also founded his own newspaper, the North Star, and served as an advisor to President Lincoln during the Civil War.

In this speech, delivered at the invitation of the Rochester Ladies' Anti-Slavery Society, Douglass powerfully illustrates the hypocrisy of asking a slave to celebrate the 4th of July. What does the 4th of July mean to a slave? asks Douglass— "a day that reveals to him, more than all other days in the year, the gross injustice and cruelty to which he is the constant victim." The following are excerpts from Douglass's original speech.

Fellow citizens, pardon me, allow me to ask, why am I called upon to speak here today? What have I, or those I represent, to do with your national independence? Are the great principles of political freedom and of natural justice, embodied in that Declaration of Independence, extended to us? And am I, therefore, called upon to bring our humble offering to the national altar, and to confess the benefits and express devout gratitude for the blessings resulting from your independence to us?

Would to God, both for your sakes and ours, that an affirmative answer could be truthfully returned to these questions! Then would my task be light, and my burden easy and delightful. For *who* is there so cold, that a nation's sympathy could not warm him? Who so obdurate and dead to the claims of gratitude, that would

Frederick Douglass 1818-1895

shame of America? "I will not equivocate; I will not excuse," I will use the severest language I can command; and yet not one word shall escape me that any man, whose judgement is not blinded by prejudice, or who is not at heart a slaveholder, shall not confess to

he is the rightful owner of his own body? You have already declared it. Must I argue the wrongfulness of slavery?...To do so would be to make myself ridiculous, and to offer an insult to your understanding. There is not a man beneath the canopy of heaven who does not know that slavery is wrong for *him*.

What, am I to argue that it is wrong to make men brutes, to rob them of their liberty, to work them without wages, to keep them ignorant of their relations to their fellow men, to beat them with sticks, to flay their flesh with the lash, to load their limbs with irons, to hunt them with dogs, to sell them at auction, to sunder their families, to knock out their teeth, to burn their flesh, to starve them into obedience and submission to their masters? Must I argue that a system thus marked with blood, and stained with pollution, is *wrong*? NO! I will not. I have better employments for my time and strength than such arguments would imply.

What then remains to be argued? Is it that slavery is not divine; that God did not establish it; that our doctors of divinity are mistaken? There is blasphemy in the thought. That which is inhuman cannot be divine! *Who* can reason on such a proposition? They that can, may; I cannot. The time for such argument is past.

At a time like this, scorching irony, not convincing argument, is needed. Oh! Had I the ability, and could I reach the nation's ear, I would today pour out a fiery stream of biting ridicule, blasting reproach, withering sarcasm, and stern rebuke. For it is not light that is needed, but fire, it is not the gentle shower, but thunder. We need the storm, the whirlwind, and the earthquake. The feeling of the nation must be quickened; the conscience of the nation must be roused; the propriety of the nation must be startled; the hypocrisy of the nation must be exposed; and its crimes against God and man must be proclaimed and denounced.

This afternoon we went to the African American Civil War Memorial. In the middle of it, there's this really neat bronze sculpture. On three sides around the sculpture is a Wall of Honor that lists all the names of the 200,000 "colored" troops that fought in the Civil War. (Colored was what black people were called a hundred years ago.)

We went into a little office where Davey and I each got a Certificate of Honor with the name of a soldier and where we could find it on the wall. Davey and I raced outside to see who could find our name first. Of course, Davey won, 'cause he got Dad to help him.

CERTIFICATE OF HONOR

Peter Godan
95th U.S. Col'd Infantry

From 1st Corps de Afrique Engineers, organized in Louisiana on April 4, 1864. This name may be located on Wall **C** Plaque **96** on the Wall of Honor at the African American Civil War Monument. The monument is located at the intersection of 10th and U Streets, N.W., Washington, D.C.

A grateful Nation finally pays tribute to the 209,145 black troops who helped save the nation, end slavery and start America on a struggle for freedom that continues today.

Dr. Frank Smith Founding Director
Civil War Memorial Freedom Foundation

For more information about this soldier visit our website address at
www.afroamcivilwar.org

This is the certificate I got.

After May 1863, when Abraham Lincoln formed the Bureau of Colored Troops, Blacks were recruited to serve in the Union Army. About 75 percent of the Blacks who fought in the Civil War were former slaves. They didn't receive equal pay, and they were given very dangerous assignments and the worst equipment.

In September 1862, Lincoln announced the Emancipation Proclamation, which abolished slavery as of January 1, 1863. I sure wanted to see the real document while we were in Washington. Mom told me it's at the National Archives Building, but it's too fragile to be put on public display.

So our trip is halfway over. Dad said the drive from Hartford to Winston-Salem is 700 miles, and we've just finished 350 miles. I can't wait to get to the family reunion to show everybody all the pictures I've taken and all the things I've collected. And, as soon as we get home, I'm going to bind all of these pages into a book and call it Sienna's Scrapbook—after me, of course! And I'll make a Memory Box, too.

July 23, Virginia

The ride from Washington, D.C., to Mount Vernon, the home of George Washington, was very short. Mom and Dad wanted us to see how slaves lived on a plantation two hundred years ago, so after we walked though Washington's BIG house, which was three stories high and had ten bedrooms (they were called bedchambers in those days) and a dining room table with enough space for twenty-four people, we went to see the slave quarters. They were so small and cramped. Our tour guide said that as many as thirty people may have slept in one room with just five bunk beds. That would make three people in each bed. How awful.

When Washington lived at Mount Vernon, he had as many as 300 slaves working for him. About a third of them were children. Until they were fourteen years old, slave children did light work around the plantation, helping their mothers prepare food or taking care of other children. After that, though, they were considered adults and were sent to work in the fields.

This is a bedroom in Washington's house.

This is the only room in a slave cabin.

Dad told me that, unlike Thomas Jefferson, George Washington freed his slaves in his will.

I asked the tour guide if the slave children ever got to play any games. "We think the boys may have played with clay marbles, because many marbles have been excavated near slave quarters here," he said. He also thought slave children may have used sticks, cornstalks, and scraps of fabric to make very simple toys, and they may have played with some of the toys belonging to the white children who visited the Washingtons.

We had a pretty big scare at Mount Vernon—we almost lost Davey. Even though I talk a lot about sending him into space, I got really scared when we couldn't find him. Mom, of course, was frantic. She yelled at Dad to run to the river to see if Davey was there, or worse, had fallen in. And, don't you know, that's exactly where he was. He'd gone to look at the boats passing by on the Potomac River. Mom and Dad both gave Davey a big hug when they found him. Then Mom gave him a *big* lecture about not wandering off.

After that excitement, we went to a tent near the entrance where there was an exhibit for kids about children's things at Mount Vernon. There was a musical instrument called a jaw harp that was used by slaves, but I sure couldn't figure it out. There was also some children's clothing that Davey and I got to try on. Of course, the dresses worn by the white children were pretty and colorful, but the ones worn by slave girls were more like drab, dull sacks. What a bummer. That is sure not my style. Give me the Gap any day!

Davey thought the hats and hoops were really cool. You roll the hoop along the ground by pushing it with the stick. The game is seeing who can keep the hoop rolling the longest. It's fun!

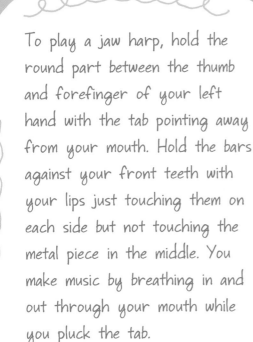

To play a jaw harp, hold the round part between the thumb and forefinger of your left hand with the tab pointing away from your mouth. Hold the bars against your front teeth with your lips just touching them on each side but not touching the metal piece in the middle. You make music by breathing in and out through your mouth while you pluck the tab.

This is a jaw harp. Believe it or not, it's a musical instrument! The guide told us that slaves may have played hand-made jaw harps. We all tried it, but the only one of us who could play it was Dad. Big surprise, huh?!

Arthur Ashe

After Mount Vernon, we were off to Richmond. Dad had heard about the statue of Arthur Ashe, the great black tennis player, and he wanted to check it out.

"Arthur Ashe was not only a great tennis player," he told us. He also wrote a huge book on the history of black athletes in America. And when he went to South Africa during the days of apartheid—that's when South Africa was segregated and Blacks there couldn't even vote— he refused to play unless black Africans were allowed to attend his matches with white Africans. What Mom remembers most about Mr. Ashe was that he had the same birthday as hers, July 10.

We found Monument Avenue, where the statue was, but all along the avenue were statues of Robert E. Lee, Jefferson Davis, and other Confederate generals. When Dad saw Mr. Ashe's statue placed on the same street with all these men who fought to keep slavery alive and well, he muttered, "There must be some better location in Richmond to honor this champion of civil rights."

We're spending the night in Richmond. Tomorrow we're going to Hampton University, where Mom and Dad went to college, fell in love, and got married about a million years ago.

Sienna the soccer champ!

July 24, Hampton, Va.

Nice hair, Dad!

"Hampton Institute was founded in 1868 as a school for the newly emancipated slaves," Dad told us as we drove onto the campus. It started out as a high school, grew into a college, and became a university in 1984. One of its most famous graduates was Booker T. Washington. Mom and Dad hadn't been back to Hampton since they were married in its Memorial Church. And, don't you know, as they showed us the church, they started holding hands and got all kissy, so Davey and I got out of there fast!

This is the church where Mom and Dad got married.

Booker T. Washington was born a slave. After emancipation, he went to school. When he was sixteen years old, he walked 500 miles from his home in West Virginia to attend the Hampton Institute. After completing his studies, he became a teacher, and in 1881, he founded the Tuskegee Institute. He was one of the foremost black educators of his time.

The campus was right on the banks of the Hampton River, so we all kept a special eye on Davey so he wouldn't wander off again. Some of the buildings are more than a hundred years old, but the most awesome thing was the Emancipation Oak, which was more than 150 years old. It was under this oak tree that the Emancipation Proclamation was read to the people of Hampton in 1863. The tree is HUGE. "The National Geographic Society has called this tree one of the ten great trees in the world," said Mom. How 'bout that!

When we got to our hotel, guess what Davey did? He ate the freeze-dried ice cream he'd bought at the Air and Space Museum. Boy, was he ever sorry! He ate too much, too fast, and had such a bad stomachache that we wound up having to stay in Hampton overnight.

The Emancipation Oak

Davey was so sick—bet he'll never eat astronaut food again!

July 25, Greensboro, N.C.

It was a long drive to Greensboro, and Davey kept asking, "Are we there yet?" He is soooooooooo annoying.

Greensboro is one of our last stops before we get to Winston-Salem. Dad wanted us to see the real Woolworth's where the student sit-ins started in 1960. But when we drove by, the Woolworth's sign was down and there were posters in the windows announcing that the building was being made into a civil rights museum. So we drove over to the North Carolina A&T campus (A&T stands for "Agricultural and Technical"), where there was a huge monument to the four students who started the sit-ins.

Then we drove to the Mendenhall Plantation in Jamestown. The plantation was built around 1811 by Richard Mendenhall, a Quaker. The family, like all Quakers, didn't own any slaves. There's a legend that they hid runaway slaves in the basement, but no one knows for sure. There's also a story that Mendenhall has a friendly ghost!

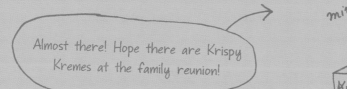

Almost there! Hope there are Krispy Kremes at the family reunion!

mine all mine!

Krispy Kreme

Out in the barn, there's this really neat wagon called a false-bottomed wagon. It was used during the days of the Underground Railroad to move slaves secretly from one station stop to another. The slaves climbed into a space between the bottom boards and the false bottom. Then the driver closed the front and back ends with sliding wooden panels, piled hay on top of the false bottom, and drove to the next stop. It must have been really scary to be traveling in that wagon at night, never knowing when slave catchers might stop the wagon.

The wagon didn't belong to the Mendenhalls, but to a family that lived nearby. Only two of these wagons are known to exist today.

Boy. So much of our history is all about the problems we faced, but as Dad says, we not only survived, we thrived. Amen to that! Our history is so rich. I wish everybody could take this awesome trip.

July 26, Winston-Salem, N.C.

We made it!!!! Krispy Kremes every day!!!! Grandma and Grandpa say they can't wait to hear about our trip. I wonder . . . maybe next summer . . . we could take another "heritage trip"?!?!

Dear Reader,

I hope you enjoyed reading about my family's trip as much as I enjoyed seeing all the sights. It really was an awesome trip!

I've made this list for you so you can find out more about the places we visited. I've included the names, addresses, phone numbers, and web sites of the places we visited. Before you travel to any of them (except for the monuments, of course), be sure you phone ahead to check on the days and hours they're open. Also, it's a really good idea to contact the visitors' bureaus in the different cities—they have up-to-date information on these locations plus more!

I've also given you information on some other places you might want to visit.

Have a great time!

Love, Sienna

BYE!!!

July 14—New Haven, Conn.

AMISTAD America, Inc.
746 Chapel Street, Suite 300
New Haven, CT 06510
Boat Dock in New Haven: 389 Long Wharf Drive
Tel: (203) 495-1839   Fax: (203) 495-9647
Toll free: (866) AMISTAD
(This teaching schooner travels to
different ports throughout the year.)
www.amistadamerica.org

July 15—New York City

Sylvia's Restaurant
328 Lenox Avenue, New York, NY 10027
Tel: (212) 996-0660   Fax: (212) 427-6389
www.slyviassoulfood.com

July 16—New York City

Louis Armstrong House
34-56 107th Street, Corona, NY 11368
Tel: (718) 478-8274
www.satchmo.net

Apollo Theater
25 West 125th Street, New York, NY 10027
Tel: (212) 531-5300   Fax: (212) 749-2743
www.apollotheater.com

ADDITIONAL SITES:

Studio Museum of Harlem
144 West 125th Street, New York, NY 10027
Tel: (212) 864-4500   Fax: (212) 864-4800
www.studiomuseum.org

The Schomburg Center for
Research in Black Culture
515 Malcolm X Boulevard
New York, NY 10037
Tel: (212) 491-2200
www.schomburgcenter.org

Abyssinian Baptist Church
132 Odell Clark Place, New York, NY 10030
Tel: (212) 862-7474   Fax: (212) 862-3255
www.abyssinian.org

July 17—Philadelphia, Pa.

The Philadelphia Doll Museum
2253 North Broad Street
Philadelphia, PA 19132
Tel: (215) 787-0220   Fax: (215) 787-0226
Email: dollmuse@aol.com
www.philadollmuseum.com

The Johnson House
6306 Germantown Avenue
Philadelphia, PA 19144
Tel: (215) 438-1768   Fax: (215) 438-5510
E-mail: info@johnsonhouse.org
www.johnsonhouse.org

July 18—Philadelphia

Mother Bethel AME Church
419 Richard Allen Avenue
Philadelphia, PA 19147
Tel: (215) 925-0616
www.MotherBethel.org

African American Museum in Philadelphia
701 Arch Street, Philadelphia, PA 19106
Tel: (215) 574-0380 Fax: (215) 574-3110
www.aampmuseum.org

ADDITIONAL SITE:

Marian Anderson Home
762 S. Marian Anderson Way
Philadelphia, PA 19146
Tel: (215) 732-9505 Fax: (215) 732-1247
www.mariananderson.org

July 19—Baltimore, Md.

Great Blacks in Wax Museum
1601-03 East North Avenue
Baltimore, MD 21213
Tel: (410) 563-3404 Fax: (410) 675-5040
www.greatblacksinwax.org

ADDITIONAL SITES:

Thurgood Marshall Monument
Edward Garmatz Federal Building (outside)
Baltimore, MD 21201
www.baltimoremd.com/monuments/thurgood.html

Benjamin Banneker Museum
300 Oella Avenue, Catonsville, MD 21228
(10 miles from Baltimore)
Tel: (410) 887-1081 Fax: (410) 203-2747
www.thefriendsofbanneker.org

July 20—Washington, D.C.

Lincoln Memorial
National Mall, Washington, DC
E-mail: National__Mall@nps.gov
www.nps.gov/nama

National Museum of American History
14th Street and Constitution Avenue, NW
Washington, DC 20560
Tel: (202) 633-1000
www.americanhistory.si.edu

July 21—Washington, D.C.

National Air and Space Museum
6th & Independence Avenue, SW
Washington, DC 20560
Tel: (202) 357-2700
www.nasm.si.edu

Mary McLeod Bethune Monument
Lincoln Park
East Capitol Street & 12th Street, NE
Washington, DC

July 22—Washington, D.C.

Frederick Douglass House
1411 W Street, SE, Washington, DC 20020
Tel: (202) 426-5961 Fax: (202) 426-0880
www.nps.gov/frdo

African American Civil War Memorial
1200 U Street, NW, Washington, DC 20001
Tel: (202) 667-2667 Fax: (202) 667-6771
E-mail: info@afroamcivilwar.org
www.afroamcivilwar.org

ADDITIONAL SITES:

Anacostia Museum & Center for African
American History and Culture
1901 Fort Place, SE, Washington, DC 20020
Tel: (202) 287-3306
www.anacostia.si.edu

Mary McLeod Bethune Council House
1318 Vermont Avenue, NW
Washington, DC 20005
Tel: (202) 673-2402
www.nps.gov/mamc

July 23—Virginia

Mount Vernon
3200 Mount Vernon Memorial Highway
Mount Vernon, VA 22121
Tel: (703) 780-2000
www.mountvernon.org

Arthur Ashe Monument
Corner of Monument Avenue and
Roseneath Road, Richmond, VA
Email: info@monumenthouse.com
www.monumenthouse.com/richmond/ashestatue

ADDITIONAL SITES:

Maggie Lena Walker House
110 1/2 E. Leigh Street, Richmond, VA 22323
Tel: (804) 771-2017
www.nps.gov/malw

Colonial Williamsburg
Carter's Grove
Williamsburg, VA 23185
Tel: (757) 229-1000
www.history.org

July 24—Hampton, Va.

Hampton University
Hampton, VA 23668
Tel: (757) 727-5000
www.hamptonu.edu

July 25—Greensboro, N.C.

Woolworth's—Civil Rights Museum
134 South Elm Street
Greensboro, NC 27420-0847
Tel: (336) 274-9199 Fax: (336) 274-6244
E-mail: info@sitinmovement.org
www.sitinmovement.org

North Carolina A&T University
1601 East Market Street
Greensboro, NC 27411
Tel: (336) 334-7500
www.ncat.edu

Mendenhall Plantation
Historic Jamestown Society, Inc.
603 West Main Street
Jamestown, NC 27282
Tel: (336) 454-3819
www.mendenhallplantation.org

Author's Note

My father, William J. Trent jr., was a member of President Franklin D. Roosevelt's historic Black Cabinet and served under Secretary of the Interior Ickes from 1936 to 1944 as Advisor on Negro Affairs. He left that position in 1944 to become the first executive director of the United Negro College Fund. In 1985, he was an honored guest at the Mary McLeod Bethune Stamp First Day Issue Ceremony in Washington, D.C., when a U.S. postage stamp was issued in her honor. And he did in fact attend the Marian Anderson concert at the Lincoln Memorial in 1939—it's his program that is reprinted in this book.

Acknowledgments

Many people can claim bits and pieces of this book—all those who shared their ideas, sent me newspaper clippings, took photographs, or drove me to sites. And I do appreciate everybody's help.

I want to start with thanks to my editor, Susan Pearson, who grabbed hold of this idea of a "heritage trip" and made it happen. And to Abby West, thanks for the "jump start!" Friends and relatives who helped: my mother, Viola Trent, and sister, Kay Holloway, Rita Rosenberg, Charlotte Holloman II, Michelle Titi, Jonathan Holloway, Jeanne Moutoussamy-Ashe, Mary Layton, Alicia Adams, Togo West, and Luke Trent Williams. And a big thanks to my dear husband, B. D. Parker Jr. (Danny to most of us), for traveling with me to some of the sites and for taking many of the photographs.

Photography Credits

Cover: Photo of Lincoln statue © iStockphoto Inc./Tom Marvin, used by permission; photo of Louis Armstrong courtesy of the Louis Armstrong House & Archives at Queens College/CUNY; National Historic Site stamp photo by Bill Clark, reprinted by courtesy of the Frederick Douglass National Historic Site; Page 9: Portrait of Margru courtesy of Beinecke Rare Book and Manuscript Library, Yale University; photos of the lazarette courtesy of Susan Pearson; Page 10: Photo of the *Amistad* under full sail © 2003 Wojtek Wacowski, used by permission; Page 15: Harlem Renaissance Map Poster Guide courtesy of Ephemera Press; cover of *Jamal's Busy Day* by Wade Hudson, illustrated by George Ford, published by Just Us Books © 1991, used by permission; Page 16: Krispy Kreme bag reprinted by permission of Krispy Kreme Doughnuts; Page 17: Photo of Sylvia Woods courtesy of the author; Page 18: Photo of Louis Armstrong courtesy of the Louis Armstrong House & Archives at Queens College/CUNY; Pages 22–23: Photos of dolls courtesy of Rita Rosenberg; photo of storefront courtesy of the author; Page 24: Photo of the split door courtesy of the author; Page 25: Photos of house interior and outbuilding courtesy of Rita Rosenberg; Page 26: Portrait of Richard Allen courtesy of Mother Bethel A.M.E. Church and Reed Photo, photo by Gary Reed; photo of church exterior courtesy of Mother Bethel A.M.E. Church; Pages 28–29: Photos of Matthew Henson, Bill Picket, and "Great Women in Civil Rights" © 2005 Jefferson Steele, used by permission; Page 31: Photo of Lincoln statue © iStockphoto Inc./Tom Marvin, used by permission; Page 32: Photo of the "I Have A Dream" step courtesy of B. D. Parker, Jr.; Page 33: Photo of Marian Anderson courtesy of University of Pennsylvania Library; Page 34: Photo of Woolworth's lunch counter courtesy of B. D. Parker, Jr.; Page 36: Photo of Tuskegee Airmen courtesy of U.S. Air Force (photo no. USAF-33267AC) via National Air and Space Museum, Smithsonian Institution; Page 37: Freeze-dried ice cream package courtesy of NASA and the Luvy Duvy Corporation, www.luvyduvy.com; Page 38: Photo of the Emancipation Statue courtesy of the author; Page 39: Photo of Mary McLeod Bethune courtesy of the National Park Service, The Mary McLeod Bethune Council House NHS, U.S. Department of the Interior; Page 40: National Historic Site stamp photo by Bill Clark, reprinted by courtesy of the Frederick Douglass National Historic Site; photo of typewriter and sewing machine courtesy of B. D. Parker, Jr.; photo of chair and clock from Frederick Douglass house brochure courtesy of the Frederick Douglass National Historic Site; Page 41: "What To The Slave Is The 4th Of July?" courtesy of the Frederick Douglass National Historic Site; Page 42: Photo of statue and Certificate of Honor courtesy of the African American Civil War Museum; Page 45: Photo of Mount Vernon bedroom by Robert C. Lautman, courtesy of the Mount Vernon Ladies' Association; photo of slave cabin interior courtesy of the author; Page 48: photo of Arthur Ashe © Jeanne Moutoussamy-Ashe, used by permission; Page 49: Photo of Arthur Ashe statue courtesy of B. D. Parker, Jr.; Page 50: Photo of Hampton University Chapel courtesy of Hampton University; Page 51: Photo of the Emancipation Oak courtesy of B. D. Parker, Jr.; Page 52: Photos of Woolworth's and the sit-in statue courtesy of Jonathan Scott Holloway; Page 54: Photos of false-bottomed wagon courtesy of Rebecca Lasley. Ticketmaster is a registered trademark of Ticketmaster Corporation.

Toni Trent Parker earned her Bachelor of Arts degree from Oberlin College and did graduate work in African American history at U.C. Berkeley. In 1992, she co-founded Black Books Galore!, through which she has organized hundreds of African American and multicultural book festivals. With her co-founders, Donna Rand and Sheila Foster, she wrote the *Black Books Galore! Guide to Great African American Children's Books* and the *Black Books Galore! Guide to More Great African American Children's Books*. Winner of Parenting magazine's Parenting Leaders Award and an NAACP Image Award finalist, Black Books Galore! has enriched the world of reading for kids of every age. The mother of three daughters, Toni is also the author of several books for children including *Hugs and Hearts, Snowflake Kisses and Gingerbread Smiles,* and *Being Me: A Keepsake Scrapbook for African American Girls*.

Janell Genovese earned her Bachelor of Fine Arts degree from Pratt Institute. Her work has since appeared in numerous magazines, including *Teen, Nick Jr., American Girl,* and *Parenting*. She is also the illustrator of *To My Sister: 100 Wishes from my Heart* by James and Lisa Grace. Janell lives in Weymouth, Massachusetts, with her husband, Jeff, and their three young children, Fiona, Shane, and Jack.

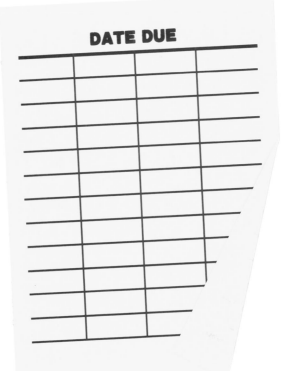